AMF

Tattoo Removal
The Low Cost Way

AMRO SOLIMA

BY

AMRO SOLIMA

Introduction

Body art evolved on its flexibility While some people take This may be because you are happy with the design

Everybody experiences a time of their lives when they understand that they have committed an error and lament their choice whether at a gathering or with a buy they have made More than likely, among around 10 million individuals holding tattoos and needs

The greater part of these number evacuated tattoos that they erroneously consented to get from the get-go in their lives

Tattoo expulsion is a system that can expel undesirable tattoos from an individual's body and it doesn't more often than not make a difference where the tattoo is on the body Tattoos can be expelled from the legs, arms, chest, neck, rear end and even the stomach This should be possible

At the point when an individual chooses to secure body workmanship, they ought to do as such while believing that body craftsmanship will consistently be In any case, here and there an individual is sick of body craftsmanship Now, they can either pick another sort of body workmanship to put on the first, or evacuate the self-perception

In the last case, it is significant that an individual locate the correct tattoo remover for their condition So as to settle on an educated choice about a tattoo remover, it is significant that the individual at any rate comprehend an essential comprehension of the tattoo life structures

At the point when a tattoo is connected to the skin, the electric needle punctures openings into the upper epidermal layers The ink goes into these openings, and bonds to the skin particles, which makes the tattoo perpetual (usually)If an individual is searching for a tattoo remover, the person in question has two primary options The main decision is having the tattoo expelled with a laser

Denton Tattoo Removal

Tattoo expulsion is an inexorably well known choice for a populace of individuals in the Denton, Texas who have as of late gotten a tattoo that they wound up lamenting Denton is a northern suburb of Dallas with numerous schools and colleges - frequently a hotspot for youngsters who get a tattoo following a night of drinking or fun with their companions

Albeit numerous tattoos are perpetual, deep rooted decorations that individuals are extremely glad and glad to have, different tattoos blur after some time, have the name of an inappropriate individual, or weren't made to be as appealing as the person or young lady were seeking after Tattoo expulsion offers these individuals an approach to expel totally or blur their undesirable tattoo With numerous individuals in Denton going to schools like Texas Women's University, the University of North Texas, and others, tattoo evacuation alternatives are critical to think about

Driving laser tattoo expulsion centers close Denton frequently get telephone approaches Monday from potential patients who got a tattoo throughout the end of the week that they aren't satisfied with This tattoo may have been gotten with sweethearts following a night of celebrating, or now and then it is a well-arranged bit of work of art that the tattoo craftsman didn't work superbly in making

Many studies point to upwards of 20% of Americans with tattoos, and even half of individuals between the age of 20 and 29 With Denton's populace more than 80,000, an unpleasant gauge may persuade that 16,000 individuals in Denton have a tattoo, however given the high centralization of schools and colleges in Denton, this number might be a lot higher

Normal tattoos that are evacuated incorporate name tattoos of an ex or ex Ladies regularly have tattoos with blooms, particularly roses, and men frequently pick innate workmanship or security fencing plans Evacuating a tattoo with a cursive or square letter name is moderately simple, particularly when the tattoo is in excess of a couple of years old or is as of now to some degree blurred

Top Ten Questions about Laser Tattoo Removal

The vast majority who are pondering evacuating an undesirable tattoo have various inquiries regarding the procedure They may have had a companion who effectively evacuated a tattoo and they need to know how it would function in their own exceptional case Or on the other hand, they may have considered tattoo expulsion numerous years prior and they need to realize what innovation is being utilized currently by tattoo evacuation facilities to make it simpler and more affordable

Tattoo expulsion specialists who have finished thousand of laser medicines have heard pretty much every inquiry you can envision about tattoo evacuation Here is a rundown of the best ten most basic inquiries concerning laser tattoo evacuation:

Can my tattoo be evacuated A vast larger part of tattoos can be expelled Dark ink (10 tattoos are the most well-known that are expelled in, and they are additionally among the least demanding to evacuate A wide scope of different hues can be expelled too - red, orange, yellow, darker green, blue, darker, purple, and hues in the middle The most troublesome hues to evacuate are light green and blue/green or blue-green or turquoise These hues can be blurred, however it is hard to expel them totally Call a facility represent considerable authority in tattoo evacuation in Dallas to become familiar with what hues are simple or difficult to expel

Is the tattoo expulsion laser perilous The medicinal laser utilized for tattoo (9 expulsion ought to be utilized only for tattoo evacuation Stay away from facilities where they utilize one laser for a wide assortment of techniques - in the same way as other things, masters have the most experience and have the most suitable hardware With appropriate security hardware (goggles to ensure the eyes), tattoo expulsion lasers are alright for use when utilized by a medicinal expert The producers of these devices go through a thorough FDA endorsement process The radiation transmitted by a tattoo expulsion laser is non-ionizing and conveys no danger of disease or other strange cell development

What sort of laser is utilized for tattoo evacuation Dallas tattoo expulsion facilities (8 use Q-exchanged Nd:YAG lasers for compelling and safe evacuation of tattoos A main brand is the Cynosure Affinity QS laser, which uses two wavelengths of light to separate the ink in a tattoo

AMRO SOLIMA

7) Will the tattoo expulsion system scar my skin Actually no, not whenever utilized by an accomplished proficient The laser doesn't make a scarring reaction by the skin when utilized by an able medical caretaker specialist, doctor colleague, or doctor Be careful about centers that utilization laser specialists who don't have propelled restorative preparing

6) How long between tattoo evacuation sessions For most patients, a month is adequate time between sessions For certain patients with brilliant, bright tattoos a month and a half is required During your meeting with a tattoo evacuation office you'll discover what might work best in your interesting circumstance

5) What conceivable symptoms will I experience For patients with dark or dim ink tattoos, some swelling and redness are the most widely recognized reactions These will typically die down inside seven days For patients with hued tattoos, some rankling may happen - this is a piece of the ordinary mending process and the skin will recuperate pleasantly thereafter

4) How does the laser separate the ink in my tattoo The laser utilizes two techniques to separate the ink - the color assimilates the vitality from the laser and is broken; the quick (6 nanosecond) heartbeat and high power of the laser will make the shade in the tattoo break separated

3) Is the laser treatment agonizing Most patients contrast the uneasiness as comparable with getting a tattoo in any case, yet a lot faster Your session may take 5-30 minutes and driving tattoo expulsion centers utilize an assortment of techniques to enable patients to confine the torment they experience

(2) what number tattoo expulsion sessions will I need Most patients will require somewhere in the range of 3 and 10 sessions The number relies upon the age of the tattoo, the hue, and the measure of ink in the tattoo Call a tattoo evacuation master to discover what you are going to need to expel your tattoo

(1) What does every session of tattoo evacuation cost The cost differs with the size of the tattoo Obviously littler tattoos will be more affordable than evacuating a whole sleeve The cost is one of various contemplations, however The nature of the medicinal staff will assume a significant job - an attendant specialist with long periods of experience and heaps of worry in helping your evacuate your tattoo will most likely expel it substantially more rapidly than somebody who is hoping to invest minimal measure of energy as would be prudent

For more data about these and different inquiries, contact a tattoo expulsion center that spends significant time in laser tattoo evacuation They'll have the option to utilize their involvement in helping you settle on an extraordinary choice in tattoo expulsion

In the event that you have a tattoo that you need evacuated for some reason, there are a few techniques accessible The greater part of them are excruciating and costly, requiring medical procedure, however there are a couple at-home evacuation options also This article will quickly depict the different systems accessible for tattoo expulsion and the estimated expense of every methodology

Laser Removal

Numerous individuals utilize the laser system to evacuate tattoos It is the most well-known strategy for expulsion, yet the drawback of the treatment is that it is excruciating, requires rehash visits, harms the skin and can cost somewhere in the range of $250 to $850 per treatment The treatment comprises of utilizing light heartbeats to separate the ink, at that point giving your body's insusceptible framework a chance to clean it up Some have depicted the impression of the procedure as having hot oil splattered on the skin Headways have been made in the innovation so next to no scarring happens, yet every case is unique Evacuating an enormous, hued tattoo can cost a huge number of dollars with this technique and albeit compelling, flawless outcomes can't be ensured

Dermabrasion

This careful strategy works only the manner in which it sounds The top layer of skin is actually "sanded" away by a turning brush that uses rough grinding It is an exceptionally agonizing procedure and neighborhood anesthesia is frequently required Swelling and scabbing of the zone is common and torment pills are frequently recommended to help with recuperation The treated region can likewise end up bothersome and balms must be connected to pick up help More than one methodology might be fundamental The middle expense of this strategy for tattoo evacuation is roughly $984 dollars

Extraction

In this surgery, the tattoo is truly removed and the skin is either sewn back together or supplanted by a skin unite cut from another piece of the body Which technique that is utilized relies upon the size of the tattoo Normally, this is an agonizing method, particularly if a skin join is vital and there for the most part is scarring The expense of this methodology changes incredibly, contingent upon what should be finished Like any surgery, the expense can be high

Extraordinary Pulsed Light Therapy

This strategy is viewed as superior to laser evacuation since it is less excruciating Gel is connected over the tattoo and a wand radiates light beats that splits up the ink much like a laser does Since it is so compelling, generally less medicines are required than with laser evacuation Shockingly, the expense of this system can be a lot higher in light of the fact that you are charged by the beat, which can be as much as $10 each In the event that your session requires various heartbeats, it can place a serious mark in your wallet or wallet

Cream Removal

On the off chance that you are worried about cost, you can attempt the at-home technique for tattoo expulsion This requires applying a cream that after some time decimates the ink underneath the skin and blurs the tattoo away Darker inks take more time to blur and the evaluated timeframe for expulsion is roughly 9 months Obviously, it shifts relying upon the tattoo and how tirelessly the creams are connected One such item that has gotten great audits is TatBGone The expense of these creams are not shoddy, however a lot less expensive than the surgeries portrayed previously Tat Gone can cost $125 for a multi month supply

Home Tattoo Removal - These Are Safety Tips You Need to Know First

Home tattoo expulsion strategies are presently a typical piece of general tattoo evacuation methods Numerous individuals need to have the option to dispose of their tattoos at home without paying so much visiting evacuation focuses This article will demonstrate to you what you have to think about expelling tattoos at home and how to do it without anyone's help

Numerous years back it used to be difficult to expel a tattoo In any case, innovation and research has throughout the years realized better approaches for expelling these tattoos, you can now effectively get these new packs and do it without anyone's help at home

Loads of individuals incline toward the non-careful home techniques in view of the chance to maintain a strategic distance from medical procedure Careful strategies can be difficult and accompanied the danger of scars, other than they are very costly as well

A portion of these outstanding careful techniques incorporate plastics medical procedure, laser tattoo evacuation, salabrasion, dermabrasion, the tissue extension strategy, cryosugrey tattoo expulsion technique and so on those recorded above are a couple of them Home tattoo expulsion has turned out to be increasingly open because of the commonness of numerous non-careful tattoo evacuation strategies

A portion of these non-careful techniques incorporates the TCA expulsion strategy, compound extraction, the infrared coagulation evacuation strategy, the tattoo blurring cream technique, the glycolic corrosive tattoo evacuation strategy, utilizing tattoo conceal and so forth These are only a couple of them

A portion of the inquiries that may consume your brain about any of the home strategies may be issues like, in the event that you can evacuate the tattoo by your self What wellbeing danger may be included

What amount such a home strategy will cost you Is there is any torment engaged with such a system In the event that it will leave a scar on your body On the off chance that there are any odds of getting tainted utilizing any of the techniques These are for the most part legitimate inquiries which you have to find solutions to

Home tattoo expulsion is a choice you ought to consider The main thing you have to do is discover increasingly about the home evacuation techniques accessible out there

AMRO SOLIMA

Tattoo Removal - Be Careful and Stay Safe With This Information

Is it accurate to say that you are going to choose a tattoo expulsion strategy Need to know what strategy is most secure and best Would you like to know whether it's something you could even do at home, all alone

In the event that you need exact responses to these inquiries and progressively about the way toward evacuating a tattoo, at that point you have to keep perusing this You are going to find the most secure and best approach to expel a tattoo without spending much or hurting yourself

For such a significant number of years individuals getting tattoos had no chance to get of successfully and easily disposing of such tattoos In any case, every one of that has changed There are currently a few different ways to evacuate those tattoos A few different ways are more secure than others

Some are extremely basic while others could leave a changeless scar on you If you don't mind note that it's significant that you pick the correct tattoo expulsion technique that suites you

The main thing you have to do is find out about the various strategies for evacuation accessible to you This is an imperative stage It would not be right of you to choose a strategy for expelling your tattoo without first instructing yourself about the various techniques and any hazard included

You have to know the advantages and disadvantages of every technique Try not to commit the lethal error of basically following the suggestion of a companion or relative Adapt more yourself

There are both careful and non careful strategies for evacuation accessible to you A portion of the outstanding careful strategies incorporate; laser tattoo evacuation, Cryosurgical tattoo expulsion, Dermabrasion expulsion, Salabrasion techniques incorporate, Excision strategy, Plastic careful, tissue extension strategy etc

Non - careful strategies incorporate; TCA tattoo evacuation, Glycolic corrosive technique, Hydroquinone strategy, IRC (Infrared Coagulation) technique, Chemical extraction strategy, the tattoo blurring cream strategy etc The rundown continues endlessly

The tattoo expulsion technique you pick shouldn't hurt you and ought to be compelling and reasonable I truly encourage you to start by discovering the best strategy for you

Tattoo Removal - Free Yourself from That Tat

So here you sit The flawless work of art you astounded him with on your last commemoration has turned into a horrendously perpetual token of your lost love Your relationship has finished; on an obnoxiously sharp note at that Presently you are looked with the cool, hard reality that perhaps you ought to have tuned in to your mom and left the ink to the biker down the road You are not the only one

AMRO SOLIMA

Today there are numerous techniques accessible to expel your obsolete craftsmanship Blur creams are most likely the main type of tattoo evacuation most of people dare to attempt By over and again slathering on blur cream, the item attempts to consistently separate the ink In the end the tattoo is rendered unrecognizable Beside moderateness, this choice is likewise very much preferred in light of the fact that it is less difficult The normal individual figures the individual has experienced enough torment as of now at first while getting the tat and after that by being placed in the position where its evacuation is esteemed fundamental

There are some tattoo expulsion alternatives, for example, dermabrasion and Sal abrasion, which include what can most effectively be clarified as sanding of the inked skin as though it were a board of wood being set up for recoloring Sanding wheels, scathing acids and salt precious stones are a couple of the parts engaged with this somewhat misleading procedure In the event that that sounds unnerving, odds are you are a run of the mill individual who takes issue to having your skin fundamentally scoured off

Another kind of tattoo evacuation that can be selected is cryosurgical tattoo expulsion This is incredible on the off chance that you like having your tissue solidified off as though you wandered out into a winter snowstorm and got a dreadful instance of frostbite That is about what it adds up to The procedure starts by solidifying the tattoo and afterward utilizing a light to make the skin strip off Sounds superb, isn't that right

In the event that you thought the last alternative for tattoo evacuation sounded somewhat absurd, you have no clue! The following kind of tattoo expulsion that is accessible for you to utilize is called extraction Think about this as exorcizing the devil that is your tattoo from your skin The tattoo is cut off of your body and the encompassing skin is gotten together like an unsettle on a prom dress and sewn together Amazing talk about truly badly arranged measures!

The last, and at present most famous, alternative for liberating your tissue from an undesirable tattoo is laser tattoo expulsion This alternative includes a progression of medicines where different lasers are centered in around the diverse tattoo colors so as to separate them and basically "break up" the tattoo from its reality There is less down time with this choice, yet for a huge tattoo, the sticker price can wind up being equivalent to purchasing a decent utilized vehicle With this alternative, "Ouch!" takes on an entirely different undertone

The lesson of this little story is: in the event that you wind up burdened with some unwelcomed ink, you have alternatives Spare the sulking for your arrival home from the tattoo parlor next go around!

Tattoo Removal - Free Yourself from That Tat

So here you sit The flawless work of art you astounded him with on your last commemoration has turned into a horrendously perpetual token of your lost love Your relationship has finished; on an obnoxiously sharp note at that Presently you are looked with the cool, hard reality that perhaps you ought to have tuned in to your mom and left the ink to the biker down the road You are not the only one

AMRO SOLIMA

Today there are numerous techniques accessible to expel your obsolete craftsmanship Blur creams are most likely the main type of tattoo evacuation most of people dare to attempt By over and again slathering on blur cream, the item attempts to consistently separate the ink In the end the tattoo is rendered unrecognizable Beside moderateness, this choice is likewise very much preferred in light of the fact that it is less difficult The normal individual figures the individual has experienced enough torment as of now at first while getting the tat and after that by being placed in the position where its evacuation is esteemed fundamental

There are some tattoo expulsion alternatives, for example, dermabrasion and salabrasion, which include what can most effectively be clarified as sanding of the inked skin as though it were a board of wood being set up for recoloring Sanding wheels, scathing acids and salt precious stones are a couple of the parts engaged with this somewhat misleading procedure In the event that that sounds unnerving, odds are you are a run of the mill individual who takes issue to having your skin fundamentally scoured off

Another kind of tattoo evacuation that can be selected is cryosurgical tattoo expulsion This is incredible on the off chance that you like having your tissue solidified off as though you wandered out into a winter snowstorm and got a dreadful instance of frostbite That is about what it adds up to The procedure starts by solidifying the tattoo and afterward utilizing a light to make the skin strip off Sounds superb, isn't that right

In the event that you thought the last alternative for tattoo evacuation sounded somewhat absurd, you have no clue! The following kind of tattoo expulsion that is accessible for you to utilize is called extraction Think about this as exorcizing the devil that is your tattoo from your skin The tattoo is cut off of your body and the encompassing skin is gotten together like an unsettle on a prom dress and sewn together Amazing talk about truly badly arranged measures!

The last, and at present most famous, alternative for liberating your tissue from an undesirable tattoo is laser tattoo expulsion This alternative includes a progression of medicines where different lasers are centered in around the diverse tattoo colors so as to separate them and basically "break up" the tattoo from its reality There is less down time with this choice, yet for a huge tattoo, the sticker price can wind up being equivalent to purchasing a decent utilized vehicle With this alternative, "Ouch!" takes on an entirely different undertone

The lesson of this little story is: in the event that you wind up burdened with some unwelcomed ink, you have alternatives Spare the sulking for your arrival home from the tattoo parlor next go around!

So here you sit The flawless work of art you astounded him with on your last commemoration has turned into a horrendously perpetual token of your lost love Your relationship has finished; on an obnoxiously sharp note at that Presently you are looked with the cool, hard reality that perhaps you ought to have tuned in to your mom and left the ink to the biker down the road You are not the only one

Today there are numerous techniques accessible to expel your obsolete craftsmanship Blur creams are most likely the main type of tattoo evacuation most of people dare to attempt By over and again slathering on blur cream, the item attempts to consistently separate the ink In the end the tattoo is rendered unrecognizable Beside moderateness, this choice is likewise very much preferred in light of the fact that it is less difficult The normal individual figures the individual has experienced enough torment as of now at first while getting the tat and after that by being placed in the position where its evacuation is esteemed fundamental

There are some tattoo expulsion alternatives, for example, dermabrasion and salabrasion, which include what can most effectively be clarified as sanding of the inked skin as though it were a board of wood being set up for recoloring Sanding wheels, scathing acids and salt precious stones are a couple of the parts engaged with this somewhat misleading procedure In the event that that sounds unnerving, odds are you are a run of the mill individual who takes issue to having your skin fundamentally scoured off

Another kind of tattoo evacuation that can be selected is cryosurgical tattoo expulsion This is incredible on the off chance that you like having your tissue solidified off as though you wandered out into a winter snowstorm and got a dreadful instance of frostbite That is about what it adds up to The procedure starts by solidifying the tattoo and afterward utilizing a light to make the skin strip off Sounds superb, isn't that right

In the event that you thought the last alternative for tattoo evacuation sounded somewhat absurd, you have no clue! The following kind of tattoo expulsion that is accessible for you to utilize is called extraction Think about this as exorcizing the devil that is your tattoo from your skin The tattoo is cut off of your body and the encompassing skin is gotten together like an unsettle on a prom dress and sewn !together Amazing talk about truly badly arranged measures

The last, and at present most famous, alternative for liberating your tissue from an undesirable tattoo is laser tattoo expulsion This alternative includes a progression of medicines where different lasers are centered in around the diverse tattoo colors so as to separate them and basically "break up" the tattoo from its reality There is less down time with this choice, yet for a huge tattoo, the sticker price can wind up being equivalent to purchasing a decent utilized vehicle With this alternative, "Ouch!" takes on an entirely different undertone

The lesson of this little story is: in the event that you wind up burdened with some unwelcomed ink, you have alternatives Spare the sulking for your arrival home from the tattoo parlor next go around!

In the event that you are thinking about tattoos, remember that they are a lasting piece of your skin Since tattoos are made with changeless ink being put underneath the skin, they are a long lasting installation except if you later choose to have them expelled Having a tattoo evacuated includes medical procedure, which is extravagant and conveys its very own dangers Similarly as with any medical procedure, there is consistently the plausibility of intricacies In the event that you are considering getting tattoos, it's ideal to ensure that you truly need them so as to abstain from having to later experience medical procedure just to expel them

Tattoos can be pricey relying upon the size of the structure They can run from the most modest of image to a huge natty gritty picture Since tattoos can be estimated high, numerous parlors offer a flighty, yet down to earth, approach to buy your plan of decision Numerous organizations offer a helpful layaway plan with the tattoos being made after the last installment is made In the event that you have the money to pay forthright, you might almost certainly make an arrangement and get the structure engraved on a similar day as installment Contingent upon the plan and multifaceted nature of the tattoos that you select, the procedure can be brief or may keep going for a considerable length of time

When thinking about tattoos, it is critical to do some exploration on the plan parlor before contracting them To what extent have they been doing business Have there been any objections held up against them with the nearby Better Business Bureau On the off chance that you have companions who additionally have tattoos, who do they prescribe and what was their experience It is critical to catch up with references and as quite a bit of a historical verification as you can get before consenting to have your tattoos made

In your exploration, attempt to discover which organizations have the best history with ensure their hardware is spotless This is the most significant interesting point about tattoos in light of the fact that, if the business isn't authorized or the craftsman is anything but an expert, there is no certification that their instruments are spotless or appropriately

Monster Tattoos - What Do Their Different Colors and Designs Really Mean

Tattoo structures are exceptionally well known these days for the two ladies and men Ladies as a rule like to have mythical beast tattoos on their foot, shoulder or arm, while men will normally get them on their back, arm or leg

Monster tattoos have a wide range of implications, differing from culture to culture A mythical beast regularly symbolizes power, mental fortitude and quality In certain societies, monsters are thought to have characteristics like astuteness, pride, power and fruitfulness and are viewed as bearers of karma In specific pieces of Asia, they frequently speak to the otherworldly power related with the water component

The prevalent hues utilized in mythical serpent plans are dark, green and red Despite the fact that mythical serpents normally inhale fire, monster tattoo plans that have a winged serpent that inhales fire are not all that normal A mythical serpent tattoo can regularly mix well with different tattoos portraying anything from skulls to blazes and wizards or images like Ying-yang and that's only the tip of the iceberg

Remember, a tattoo is agonizing and costly to evacuate, in this way, it is significant you require some investment when picking your winged serpent plan When scanning the web for monster tattoo pictures and workmanship, individuals will in general select the free plans Thusly, they frequently commit a major error Free plans are frequently of low quality Considering that a tattoo is a perpetual masterpiece, you ought not go out on a limb of being left with a poor plan that you will most likely wind up lamenting There are different methods for discovering tattoo plans these days Among the most well known sources are books and magazines Most decent book shops include a wide range of magazines and books with numerous photographs of plans Other significant assets are tattoo parlors; tattoo shows are likewise extraordinary on the grounds that you get the chance to talk with the specialists themselves and approach them for their thoughts or help in planning your winged serpent tattoo Be that as it may, the most advantageous asset is, no ifs, ands or buts, the web The web enables you to peruse a large number of structures whenever it might suit you from the solace of your home

When scanning for a tattoo structure, it is essential to recall that you get what you pay for In the event that a structure is free it is most possibilities are it was finished by an unpracticed craftsman The structure will be far beneath the nature of a tattoo planned by an expert craftsman Keep in mind: expelling a tattoo is excruciating and costly, so ensure you take when scanning for your ideal mythical beast tattoo

Tattoo Care - 10 Sizzling Tips on Tattoo Care

Tattoo care is One of the absolute last things that somebody ponders as they choose to get a tattooTattoo care is a prerequisite, particularly on the off chance that you hope to protect your tattoo for any degree of time It has regularly been said that the underlying week is the most significant for recuperating, however it is extremely the initial 4 to about a month and a half The means that you take so as to think about your tattoo will be noteworthy with respect to shielding it from getting to be contaminated

Here are a few hints that will be important in thinking about your new tattoo

1 Keep in mind your tattoo craftsman's definite guidance on tattoo care when you leave their shop after accepting your new tattoo Most craftsman's can record or as of now have existing exhortation and tips on tattoo care, so simply make certain that you inquire

2 Comprehend that you are at a hazard for contamination on the off chance that you don't oblige the bearings When your tattoo gets contaminated, at that point you will be in risk A contaminated tattoo can incredibly protract the mending procedure and make everything quite a lot more awkward than it as of now is

3 Legitimate tattoo care expects you to Wear your swathe Ask your tattoo craftsman precisely to what extent the person in question prescribes that you wear it A few

people should basically wear their wraps for close to 24 hours while others need to wear them any longer It just relies upon how responsive your skin is, the amount it is parted from the tattoo, and how huge your tattoo is Regardless, ensure that you wear it; it will keep contamination from emerging

Verify that when you are washing your tattoo, that you wash with tepid water, or the hottest water that you can take at the time

Expel the blood with your hands when washing the tattoo, not a wash material A wash material can be a lot and can make disturbance the skin It is ideal to keep those hints of blood expelled so as to avert superfluous scabbing

Try not to pick at it This may cause injuries and all the more dying, which could prompt disease Simply make sure to keep it clean

Fend off it from salt water and daylight until it has mended You don't need your tattoo to blur or harm in any capacity Also that if you somehow managed to do possibly, it would hurt to excess

Remember to apply balm Ask your tattooist which treatment is prescribed for greatest mending Keep the salve connected, and don't quit applying until your tattooist gives the alright

Abstain from cleaning up and showers You don't need your new gem to lose any ink Concentrate on scrubbing down

Fend off every single other synthetic from your tattoo, even cleanser Try not to 10 endeavor to wash it or shave it On the off chance that you use shaving cream, make certain to apply the cream around the tattoo An excessive number of synthetics can demolish it It for the most part takes somewhere in the range of 4 to about a month and a half to mend When it has mended, at that point you are allowed to sunbathe, wash up, showers, or whatever else you want to do

With the right tattoo care your tattoo will be okay, yet like whatever else that is in a mending procedure, extraordinary consideration is required You may even need to keep on applying cream to it for some time just to ensure that the skin remains soggy, crisp, and does not break or strip excessively A tattoo is a wise speculation regardless of what way you take a gander at it Appropriate tattoo care is the best thing you can accomplish for your venture, and for your skin

Microdermabrasion

Microdermabrasion is a nonintrusive healthy skin system that has relentlessly developed in prominence in the course of recent years The manner in which it works is extremely basic - a machine is utilized to expel the highest layer of skin to dispose of dead skin cells and clear up and treat the skin

Commonly, a machine is utilized which acts both to "impact" aluminum oxide precious stones onto the skin and suck up utilized gems and dead skin cells The outcomes are dazzling and moment - immediately you will see that your skin has a fresher look, and an increasingly brilliant sparkle to it

It will likewise decrease the measure of harm done by sun to your skin, diminish wrinkles and scarcely discernible differences, treat your pores and de-surface your skin, leaving you with a smooth surface and an energetic appearance

Microdermabrasion has additionally been alluded to as "control stripping" or molecule reemerging The entire procedure is exceptionally straightforward and just takes you 20 to 30 minutes to finish it A while later, there is no down time for recuperation, and you're ready to approach your typical course

Normally, medications are given in an arrangement, and the value range goes from as low as $75 per session to upwards of $200 Presently, the national normal is $135 per session In any case, in the event that you complete a progression of sessions you may get a limited rate Additionally, your expense per session will rely on where you live

This procedure isn't difficult by any stretch of the imagination, and no nearby anesthesia is required to provide for the patient On the off chance that the patient's skin is touchy, at that point more medicines might be expected to accomplish attractive outcomes

The main safety measure you have to apply after your treatment is to ensure you avoid broadened introduction from the sun, and that you apply sunscreen, and ensure the majority of the dead skin cells and aluminum oxide precious stones have been expelled from your skin

At last, remember to investigate the home choices that are accessible to you with regards to this treatment procedure There are currently wide range of home treatment cares which incorporate a microdermabrasion instrument, tool cushion, and precious stone cream which are utilized related to treat the skin

All in all, I have given you some data about what microdermabrasion is, just as a portion of the advantages and costs that are related with this procedure

Dealing with Your Tattoo Art

There are various manners by which tatoo evacuation works There are a few thoughts that have been around for quite a long time, while others are simply starting to pick up noticeable quality Every one of the evacuation choices will be agonizing, and some case that it is similarly as difficult as getting the tatoo itself This is on the grounds that the it ventures down into a few layers of skin, and every one of these layers must be expelled The various techniques must venture into each layer of skin to completely evacuate

The principal sort of evacuation includes the utilization of lasers Laser expulsion is the most prominent structure accessible today It has been around since the 1980's, yet its prevalence has just developed as of late There are even workplaces that exist just to utilize this kind of laser innovation With this kind of method, a low level laser is pointed straightforwardly at the skin The throbbing laser at that point gradually swamps off the tattoo until it vanishes totally This may take a few sessions spread out more than half a month or even months On the off chance that the tatoo is bigger it might require some investment for the procedure to work

Another sort of method is dermabraison Numerous individuals know this methodology as a restorative strategy that removes layers of dead skin to make the skin look more youthful and increasingly solid As a type of tattoo expulsion, it works similarly A desensitizing ointment or cream is connected legitimately to the skin in the area of the tattoo A little machine that seems to be like a little sanding belt is then scoured against the skin This gradually separates the ink and sands off the layers of skin Now and again the specialist may solidify the skin first before doing this evacuation methodology

One of the more extraordinary types of evacuation is known as extraction With this methodology the tatoo is actually removed the skin The skin is then sewn back set up and permitted to recuperate This lone works with extremely little tattoos, and in individuals with exceptionally flexible skin

Expulsion alternatives can without much of a stretch be found by looking in the telephone directory or on the web The expense of such systems relies upon the hues utilized in the tattoo, the size, and here and there the area The individual who handles the evacuation procedure can offer more data just as an accurate expense of the method

Made in the USA
Las Vegas, NV
01 March 2022